M000224438

PUSH

A 21 DAY CHALLENGE

For Spiritual Growth

Get ready to push!

[signature]

4 - 2021

~ Where will I Live?

~ Where will I go to
church and be
planted?

~ What work of the
ministry am I
to be apart
of?

IVY SMITH

Like a Woman in Travail, Get Ready to Push!

Push

Trilogy Christian Publishers A Wholly Owned Subsidiary of Trinity Broadcasting Network 2442 Michelle Drive Tustin, CA 92780

Copyright © 2020 by Ivy Smith

Scripture quotations marked KJV are taken from the King James Version of the Bible. Public domain.

Scripture quotations marked NLT are taken from the Holy Bible, New Living Translation, copyright © 1996, 2004, 2015 by Tyndale House Foundation. Used by permission of Tyndale House Publishers, Inc., Carol Stream, Illinois 60188. All rights reserved.

No part of this book may be reproduced, stored in a retrieval system, or transmitted by any means without written permission from the author. All rights reserved. Printed in the USA. Rights Department, 2442 Michelle Drive, Tustin, CA 92780.

Trilogy Christian Publishing/TBN and colophon are trademarks of Trinity Broadcasting Network.

For information about special discounts for bulk purchases, please contact Trilogy Christian Publishing.

Trilogy Disclaimer: The views and content expressed in this book are those of the author and may not necessarily reflect the views and doctrine of Trilogy Christian Publishing or the Trinity Broadcasting Network.

Manufactured in the United States of America

10 9 8 7 6 5 4 3 2 1

Library of Congress Cataloging-in-Publication Data is available.

ISBN: 978-1-64773-739-9

E-ISBN: 978-1-64773-740-5

Table of Contents

Purpose

Through this twenty-one-day challenge, it is my prayer that you will experience the holy presence of God on a daily basis. I pray that you will experience spiritual growth, while learning to listen to God's whispers, nudges, and even His *pushes*. In this selfie-saturated, Insta-this, Insta-that world, it's hard to find that quiet time with the Lord. It's time to block out the noise of social media, step away from your responsibilities for just fifteen minutes a day, for twenty-one days, and spend much needed quality time with the Lord. You see, God longs for time with you. Your days may be demanding and stressful and sometimes even downright hectic. In the midst of it all, He wants to help you get through the chaos; you just have to let Him.

So, let's dive into this book with just a few minutes a day, spending time with God through prayer, reading His word, and praising Him. I recommend getting up fifteen to twenty minutes before your daily routine starts, finding a quiet space, putting on praise music, and starting each morning with the Lord. When the book is over, I hope you will have a routine of spending your mornings with the Lord. After you settle into this routine, I believe you will be better equipped to handle the chaos and stress of everyday life. This book will be like a spiritual boot camp or a spiritual diet, so to speak. It's time to trim the fat, purge the junk from your life, and draw closer to God. So, no excuses. Chasing Christ has to be a priority for all of us. God wants our first fruits. I believe that is not only our tithe but also our time. God craves time with you. When you set aside specific time with the Lord, the rest of your time will be blessed. So, take these twenty-one days to get in a routine of spending time with the Lord and get ready to push.

Preface

Hello there! Let me introduce myself. My name is Ivy Smith. I am first and foremost a child of the one true King, Jesus Christ, my Lord and Savior. I am also a wife to an amazing husband, David, and mother of two beautiful boys, Gabriel and Samuel. I am not a preacher or teacher; I am simply a woman after God's heart, seeking His will for my life. A few years ago, God placed a yearning in my heart to minister to others; yet, at the time, I didn't know how He wanted me to do that. In hindsight, I believe He was nurturing me to the place He needed me to be in order to carry out His will.

We all experience different seasons in our lives: some hard, some easy, and some unexplainable. For several years, I dealt with depression and anxiety. My anxiety was so bad that it interfered with my daily life. I had a newborn and didn't want to leave the house. I was in serious trouble. There were days I didn't want to do anything or see anyone. Finally, I woke up one day to the realization that the devil was robbing me of the life God had planned for me. I knew God didn't want this for my life, yet I didn't know how to get to the place of peace the Bible talked about. I wanted peace. With everything that was in me, I wanted to do what it was going to take to get there. So, I started a routine. Every morning, I got up, drank my coffee, turned on Christian music, read my Bible, and prayed. My daily prayer during this time was that I would have God's true peace, joy, and abundance. The anxiety and worry became less and less every day. I truly began to find my confidence in who I was as a child of God. I started experiencing His presence like never before. I cannot express how wonderful I began to feel, just an absolute high on Jesus. I could experience God in so many powerful ways, in my own time, not just at church. This was a new revelation to me, and I wanted to share it with everyone!

My church started a fast in January of 2019. During the first week of the fast, the Lord stirred in my spirit the message for this book. He then gave me the name for it, but that was about it. I didn't know exactly how it would be written or when, all I knew was that He was stirring something fresh in me. I sensed a hunger in my belly and craved that next level of revelation.

I soon found out I was pregnant with our second son, Samuel. I was physically and spiritually pregnant with new life. But just as there was an incubation period for my baby, there was also an incubation period for what God was stirring in me spiritually. Other than the name of the book and general message, the Lord had yet to lay any revelations on my heart. I was ready to write but had no insight.

A few months later, I prayed about the book one Sunday morning before church. During service that Sunday, a lady came up to me and stated the Lord told her that I was physically and spiritually pregnant. She had no clue what I was walking through or that the Lord had given me this book to write. She said, "I don't know if God wants you to write a book or what, but He says that you are physically pregnant and spiritually pregnant with a ministry." So, there it was. God gave me confirmation through her. How powerful was that? It was still months later before God had me write this book, but we must understand that our timing is not God's timing.

After I gave birth to Samuel, I finally felt God moving in my spirit to write *Push*. Before He gave me the content for the first challenge day, He whispered to my spirit, "You can't write it until you're ready to walk it." Ouch! That stung. I had an overwhelming wave of conviction. This was the exact reason why He hadn't given me anything to write sooner. I wasn't spiritually lined up with Him. God is a God of order, and I had to come under His order to walk out His will. I had to come to the spiritual level needed to start this journey and get rid of some ugly things in my heart.

I began asking God to reveal to me what I needed to change to do His will. He revealed I had been holding on to unforgiveness and resentment. Boy, I needed to repent! The conviction was strong, and the truth stung a little. Okay, actually, it stung a lot. It was easy for me to point out flaws in others, but when I had to look at my own heart, I'd rather run in the other direction. Have you ever felt that way? After having this conviction, I humbly repented, and I felt as if my spirit grew wings!

Repentance is so critical in our walk with God. It keeps us in line and holds us accountable. It's where the action starts and God sees we're willing. It's where we can make leaps in our Christian walk. God had me start with repentance. In order for me to write, I had to experience repentance first!

The focus of this book is to cut off the flesh and grow in the spiritual. I don't want you to think this book is beating you up, but if you want to grow in your walk with Christ, you need to complete this book. Take these next few weeks to examine your heart, explore the revelations God showed me, and remove spiritual hindrances. It's truly amazing what God will reveal to us, if we would be willing to listen to His *pushes*.

As you commit to this twenty-one-day journey, get ready to cut off those fleshly desires and listen to the pushes of the Holy Spirit. Pray those specific prayers and spend time with Him. Complete this spiritual challenge and watch God change your life like He has mine!

Day 1: The Heart Work

Today's Reading: Matthew 6 (KJV)

Selected Verse for Today:

For where your treasure is, there will your heart be also.

Matthew 6:21 (KJV)

To start writing this book, I had to make a heart change. One day as I was praying about this book, God quickened my spirit and flatly said, "In order to write this book you have to walk it first." Wow! Just, Wow! I was shaken but in a good way. This truth hit me hard though. I knew I had a choice to make. I chose God. Over everything else, I listened to the quickening of the Holy Spirit. I repented of the ugly in my heart. I realized that I had allowed bitterness into my heart, and I had to make a serious change. I had to let go of resentment, anger, and unforgiveness.

Have you ever held onto a few things you knew you needed to let go of? Have you ever allowed the enemy to take your joy and then blamed it on your situation or someone else? Well, I have. That's where I was, and boy, did I have to make a change. I had allowed the enemy to set up camp in my heart. But once I repented, I felt as if chains fell off. I took back what the devil tried to keep from me: my joy. I decided to take that leap and jump for Jesus like never before! I made the choice to push the ugly out of my heart and allow God to birth something new in me! So, are you ready to walk this out, too? Are you ready to push out the ugly in your heart and receive fresh fire from the Holy Spirit? I hope and pray so. Let's get started!

Today, read Matthew 6 and study the scriptures. Ask the Lord to give you fresh insight through the scriptures. Mull them over in your spirit and grind on them all day. Seek God and pray. Ask him to forgive you of your known sins and reveal to you what you need to change. Ask Him to show you the ugly, the things you've buried deep, or didn't realize were there. Ask God to help open your eyes to what you've turned a blind eye to. Ask Him to open your ears to the sound of His voice, His convictions, and His pushes. And be ready to sit down when you hear Him respond to you! Then, take a deep breath and repent. With your whole heart, repent.

At every doctor's visit during pregnancy, a doctor or nurse places a heartbeat monitor on the expecting mother's stomach. Within seconds, she hears the life and heartbeat of the baby growing inside of her. That feeling is indescribable. She can hear the baby's kicks, rolls, and other movements. Most importantly, she can hear the baby's heartbeat. The rhythm of the baby's heartbeat races as it adjusts to the frequency of the monitor. Hearing her baby move around inside of her is a special experience. Knowing that God placed that baby inside of her is incredibly amazing. I remember, on a few occasions, during my own pregnancy doctor's visits, the heartbeat monitor came back empty until the nurse located the correct spot to hear my baby's heartbeat. Those few moments were terrifying. But sure enough, the sound of my baby's movements and heartbeat came booming through the monitor. I thank the Lord for His peace that rushed over me during those doctor's visits.

Our spiritual journey is a lot like pregnancy and motherhood. The trials that come with pregnancy and motherhood can be hard but well worth it. Once the baby is born, it is like a prize. It is utterly amazing to know you sacrificed your body to bring a child into this world. Our spiritual journey often reflects the same pattern. We may go through trials that seem to draw the life out of us, but then there is Jesus holding us up, and our faith grows deeper in those times.

When we are pregnant with God's will, our spiritual life will blossom and grow. God may be birthing something new inside of you literally or spiritually, but if your heart doesn't line up with His will, you may miss it. You may miss out on what God wants to birth inside of you due to spiritual hindrances. You have to learn to push out the junk that doesn't need to be in your life, to birth what God has planted inside of you. So, first you have to confront what is hindering you from growing spiritually. If someone could place a "spiritual monitor" on you, what would your monitor sound like? Would it have a healthy heartbeat or send back a soundless void?

We all fall short of the glory of God, but because of God's grace, we can confess our sins and move forward. So, before we go to work on this twenty-one-day challenge, we have to examine everything in our briefcase.

How heavy is your briefcase? What are you carrying around with you every day? I know these are hard questions, but if you genuinely want more of God, you must address them. Sly little "baby sins" may be lurking the corner, but whatever they are, you are never beyond God's grace. His grace is sufficient, and He says His mercies are new every morning. Amen for that! It's easier to turn the other way when our hearts are convicted. Don't turn away! Don't ignore or even overlook the smallest of things because they could keep you from growing deeper. God knows all. He is omniscient. You don't have to hide your faults. He knew the decisions you would make before you were even born. When you are faithful to examine your heart, repent, and return to Him, He will reward you.

I know this will be the hardest part of this spiritual challenge. No one likes to look in the mirror or at their inward self. In today's society, everyone is so focused on their outward appearance, how many "friends" they have on social media, how many times their posts got "liked," and what the world thinks about them. None of these matter to God. The Lord looks at the heart. The Bible says, "...for the Lord seeth not as man seeth; for man looketh on the outward appearance, but the Lord looketh on the heart" (1 Samuel 16:7, KJV).

As I was starting this very page, I was reminded of something from church. All the women participated in a secret sister exchange. We filled out forms to be paired with someone. One of the questions on the sheet asked us to list our favorite scripture verse. I immediately wrote Matthew 6:21. It has been one of my favorite scripture verses for so long. In this scripture Jesus says, "For where your treasure is, there your heart will be also" (Matthew 6:21, KJV). This passage where Jesus is speaking is profound to me. He also says, "Lay not up for yourselves treasures upon earth, where moth and rust doth corrupt, and where thieves break through and steal. But lay up for yourselves treasures in heaven, where neither moth nor rust doth corrupt, and where thieves do not break through nor steal" (Matthew 6:19-20, KJV). This is the ultimate! I want to shout when I read this passage, because of its profound truth! It's like a weighted bomb that hits me in the gut. Jesus is my treasure! There is nothing on this earth that will satisfy like the love of Jesus.

As I began facing the carnal flaws I had in my heart, God began to soften my spirit. I became quite hardened to the world and people around me. I let everyday responsibilities weigh me down to the point that it was affecting my attitude and relationships. I did'nt project the joy of the Lord. I projected negativity and criticism, and, frankly, I was cranky! I was ready for God to be my joy. I needed God to change my heart. I was just so caught up in the noise around me that I wasn't listening to the Holy Spirit. It's easy to get caught up in the natural, and before we realize it, we've gone days, weeks, months, and even years without really being the Christ-like image we were made in.

Jesus said, "But thou, when thou fastest, anoint thine head, and wash thy face; That thou appear not unto men to fast, but unto thy Father which is in secret: and thy Father, which seeth in secret, shall reward thee openly" (Matthew 6:17-18, KJV). Fasting is a form of spiritual discipline while pushing down the lust of the flesh. Now, I'm not calling upon you to fast food but to fast a few minutes of your time. Ignore the call of the natural world and devote a certain amount of your time to God every day, and He will reward you openly. I'm not talking about material rewards. Your countenance will begin to change, and people will take notice. This is where your foundation is built. Your life is a reflection of you. So, what does your life say about your foundation? Does it look strong in the Lord or weak from your circumstances? This is where we start. This is where God had me start: the foundation of my heart.

I know today's challenge is long. It is the longest challenge in the book, but our foundation must be solid so that it's immovable. Let's face the ugly, the negative, and even the painful. Let's do the heart work.

In the last section of today's challenge, I want you to pour out your heart. Write down everything that God reveals to you, write down your convictions and what you know you need to work on. At the end of this twenty-one-day challenge, refer back to this page and do a heart check.

Let's Pray.
Dear Heavenly Father,
I thank you for your glory, Lord. I thank you for your matchless grace and mercy. I thank you for your love. Change my heart, oh God. Reveal to me that which I need to change. Help me to see clearly. Manifest your presence in my life everyday so that I may know you more. I seek you right now, Father. I yearn to grow deeper in you, Lord. Give me a pure heart and clean hands. I want to change. Release from me what is holding me back from knowing you more. Help me to hear you and live by your convictions. And release off of me any baggage that is pulling me down. Give me a heart change. I want a fresh start with you, Lord. Amen.

Day 1 is done; your beautiful journey has begun! Today is one of the hardest days, but now it's behind you! Let go of the old, because God is going to birth something new in you, amen!

Write down what's on your heart right now:

_____

_____

_____

_____

_____

_____

_____

_____

Day 2: Soul Conversion

Today's Reading: Psalms 19

Selected Verse for Today:

The law of the Lord is perfect converting the soul: the testimony of the Lord is sure, making wise the simple.

Psalms 19:7 (KJV)

Welcome to Day 2! In preparation for today's message, the Holy Spirit led me to Psalms 19. It resounded in my spirit for several days before He gave me what I wrote. What He gave me for today ministered to me in a powerful way. I hope and pray it will minister to your spirit also.

When you seek God with your whole heart, He begins to shape and mold you into something you never imagined. Chains begin to fall off, thoughts begin to change, and before you know it, you are made new. You are converted. Through accepting Jesus as your Savior, receiving the Holy Spirit, and proclaiming God as your King, you are ultimately and profoundly made into a new creation. You begin to let go of past sins, mistakes, regrets, shame, unforgiveness, etc. God's convictions convert your heart. You start to see things you need to change about yourself that maybe you didn't see before or didn't want to confront. God says today, keep pushing, you're in a transformation process. As hard as it may be, the transformation will be worth it!

If you have insecurities hindering your marriage, a rotten attitude, jealousy, or any bitterness, this transformation is for you! If you need to let go of anger, gossip, or back-biting, then keep pushing! If you're mad at your neighbor or co-worker, keep pushing! If you've allowed circumstances that are out of your control to dictate who you've become, then keep pushing! Push, woman! Push the ugly out!

I had to come to a hard realization that I didn't even like being in the same room with myself, and that was utterly devastating to face. I allowed my circumstances to make me bitter. But what I needed was to become better!

It is so hard to apologize when you've done wrong, that's just human nature. Trust me, I had a lot of apologizing to do! I had to repent and change the way I acted towards my husband, my kids, and everyone else. I had a lot to work on! But you know what, as I began to change, I felt a literal shift in the atmosphere around me.

Something you don't realize is that your attitudes, actions, and words can affect your atmosphere. You can make and create the air of your surroundings. For me, the air in my home began to stink because of my rotten attitude! I was snappy and begrudging. I had a lot of offenses I needed to get rid of. I had to stop myself many times from going on the offensive about every little thing. Ever been there before? I was allowing the devil to rob my joy! So, by the time God revealed to me the things I needed to change, I was ready. I needed Him more than ever. I needed a transformation. I needed a soul conversion.

During pregnancy, your body begins to take a different shape because there is a new life growing inside of you. The Lord says today is the day that you start taking a different form. Day One was all about a heart examination and letting go of known sins. Today, God takes you one step further into secret faults and reveals what is hidden to have a true conversion. Today is the day you commit to doing things God's way not because you think you have to, but because you want to. You want true soul conversion so that you can morph into the woman God has called you to be!

Let's start today by trying to recognize things in your life that don't belong and cut them off. The Bible says, "Who can understand his errors? Cleanse thou me from secret faults. Keep back thy servant also from presumptuous sins; let them not have dominion over me: then shall I be upright, and I shall be innocent from the great transgression" (Psalms 19:12-13, KJV). Don't allow your circumstances to make you bitter. Bitterness will only cause you to sin more, hindering your relationship with God and everyone else around you. And a hindered relationship will allow the enemy to have dominion over you. "Dominion" is a powerful word. You don't realize how much power you give to things to have over you. Do you have anything in your life that you need to change that has dominion over you? Maybe you don't consider it to be a sin, but you know it causes a hindrance in some way. Whatever it may be, if you are convicted about it, honor that conviction.

Ask God to help you have self-control and be ready to let go of things that you've allowed to have dominion over your life. Ask God to continue to change you. Sometimes God will ask us to do things that our flesh isn't ready to do. I want to always be obedient to His will, because that's where His glory is! Do you want to see His glory in your life? Seek to be all that He wants of you. Even though you will make mistakes along the way, thank Jesus for His grace.

So today, seek God. Be reminded that His law is perfect, even when you are not. Seek to obey Him. Seek to grow closer to Him through your words, thoughts, and actions. The Bible says, "Let the words of my mouth and the meditation of my heart, be acceptable in thy sight, O Lord, my strength and my redeemer" (Psalms 19:14, KJV) Let God be your strength, to help you overcome your secret faults. Let Him be your righteousness. I promise He will give you His grace; your job is to reach out and grab it!

Today, read Psalms 19. Meditate on His love, and it will sweep over you like a rushing wave. Throughout the day, when you feel overwhelmed or when you are reminded of your faults, ask God for His grace to transform you.

Paul wrote, "And be not conformed to this world: but be ye transformed by the renewing of your mind, that ye may prove what is that good, and acceptable, and perfect, will of God" (Romans 12:2, KJV). Be strong in the Lord. Try not to feel overwhelmed or condemned. Ask the Holy Spirit to renew your mind and spirit through this journey and He will.

Let's Pray.
Dear Heavenly Father,
I seek you today, Lord, for your glory to overwhelm me. Show me your ways. Reveal to me what you want me to shake off. Cut off from my life those secret sins and faults. Lord, I love you and seek your righteousness. Forgive me of my sins. Help me to be obedient to your word. Renew my mind. Help me to be upright. Give me a true soul conversion today, Lord, so that I may be a walking example of your love and grace. In your name I ask, Jesus. Amen.

Day 2 is done! Take a sigh of relief. Meditate on God's word, love, and grace to help you change today. Continue to transform. Push, woman! You've got this!

DAY 2: SOUL CONVERSION

List things you can change for a true conversion:

_____

_____

_____

_____

_____

_____

_____

_____

Day 3: Finding God in the Wilderness

Today's Reading: Psalms 63

Selected Verse for Today:

When I remember thee upon my bed, and meditate on thee in the night watches.

Psalms 63:6 (KJV)

Before David reigned as king, he was on the run for his life for several years from King Saul. The Bible says that he and his men encamped in the wilderness with little food and resources. He even had to leave his wife. Samuel had already anointed David as the next king, so why did God allow this to happen? God was strengthening David in the wilderness not to rely on man but on God himself.

The Bible refers to the wilderness as a time of testing, and it was a time of testing for David. Jesus was tested in the wilderness for forty days by Satan. The Bible even says that the spirit drove Jesus into the wilderness, but while He was there, the angels ministered to Him. At the end, He was found faithful. The wilderness is a theme that runs throughout the Bible in several popular stories. Remember the Israelites were sent into the wilderness for forty years after Moses led them out of captivity in Egypt? However, the Bible tells us that an entire generation of Israelites died off while in the wilderness because of their complaining. Even though they wandered for so long, they weren't physically far from their promised land. Because they chose to question God and complain, they missed His promise for forty years. How you respond in those wilderness seasons is so important. It will determine what comes next in your life. Do you ever feel as if you're in a wilderness season of some sort? How do you respond to those times of testing? Would God find you faithful or complaining as the Israelites did?

Even though wilderness seasons are the hardest to endure, they are usually where you experience God the most. Finding God in the middle of the wilderness is sweet and satisfying. I would walk out ten thousand trials to draw closer to God. His grace and mercy will cover us and strengthen us during those times. When you feel as if you are being attacked or chased down by the enemy, God will meet you right there where you are and minister to you exactly what you need to get through that season. Take those seasons to meditate on God and allow Him to shape you into the creation He has called you to be. Humble yourself before Him. Meditate on Him in the "night watches," in the wee hours of the morning, and He will cover you with His love and peace.

When I was pregnant with our second son, Samuel, my skin broke out with an awful rash. It itched severely. It was so severe at night that I could barely sleep. I scratched until the rashes bled. I needed relief. During the night, I found myself crying out to God to take the itch away and to help me sleep. There is nothing like a physical ailment that's relentless. But during this time, it strengthened my relationship with the Lord. I sought his face in those overwhelming moments. His peace that surpasses all understanding came down and covered me like the dew of heaven. If you're in need of His peace during a season of wilderness, meditate on Him. He will meet you right where you are and be your strength.

Today, read Psalms 63 and meditate on the Lord. If you aren't in a season of testing, pray for others that may be in a wilderness season.

Let's Pray.
Dear Lord,
Thank you for your love and mercy. Your joy is my strength in times of testing. I seek you today, Lord. Minister to me during this season and show me your ways. I pray for those who may also be experiencing a season of testing that you will minister to them. Give us a sound mind, Lord and continue to grow us spiritually. Holy Spirit, guide

me through this season and manifest in my life. I seek you today, Lord. In Jesus name I ask, amen.

Day 3 is over, and I hope it ministered to you. No matter what you face, God will lead you through. Meditate on Him in those wilderness seasons for that is where you will see Him move so profoundly in your life.

Write down things you can do in times of testing:

_____

_____

_____

_____

_____

_____

_____

_____

_____

Day 4: Waiting on the Lord

Today's Reading: Psalms 27

Selected Verse for Today:

Wait on the Lord: be of good courage, and he shall strengthen thine heart: wait, I say, on the Lord.

Psalms 27:14 (KJV)

God's timing is impeccable. It cannot be altered, replaced, or achieved except by Him. So many times we want to jump the gun, take matters into our own hands, and say "I've got this" without regard to God's will for our lives. We love to be in control; it's our human nature. We need to learn how to forfeit to God. Forfeiting isn't a bad thing, not giving into God is.

As a parent, I want what is best for my children. I want them to listen to correction in order to instill good values and Christian beliefs into them. I want them to be good, kind, and loving. I want to teach them the difference between right and wrong. I know that as they get older, I will be teaching them different things. I know my son, Gabriel, is very impatient. He often doesn't want to listen when I call out his name or do what I ask him to do. I get so frustrated with him, especially since I know he knows better. It's the same thing with our Heavenly Father. He wants to ensure that His children are getting what they need through correction, conviction, and certain seasons. But when you don't listen to Him or wait on His answer, you can get frustrated and take matters into your own hands. This is where you mess up. Can you imagine how frustrated God gets with us? Yet somehow, He extends His grace and His mercy.

Instead of waiting on God to give you what you want, you should be waiting on God to give you what He knows you need. It is His ultimate plan that has your best interests in mind, and His plan that works out miracles in your life.

As I wrote, God led me to this passage that says, "It is of the Lord's mercies that we are not consumed, because his compassions fail not. They are new every morning: great is thy faithfulness. The Lord is my portion, saith my soul; therefore will I hope in him. The Lord is good unto them that wait for him, to the soul that seeketh him" (Lamentations 3:22-25, KJV). The Lord is your portion, hallelujah! Shout that one out! Don't grow weary in well doing but keep the hope of the Lord. Seek Him all the days of your life, and His will shall come to pass, even when you think it may not. Wait on His answer, not yours. For His answers are perfect. So, hope while you wait. Seek Him and you will find Him. His peace will surpass all of your misunderstandings while in the waiting. Allow His strength and mercy to cover you in those relentless moments. Allow His grace to minister to you in moments you feel like giving up. Be hopeful in affliction. Be hopeful in trying times. Be hopeful in the waiting. Without hope, you wither away. Do not lose hope. And keep pushing, my friend, you've got this! Meditate on Psalms 27 and be encouraged.

Let's pray.
Dear Lord,
Help me today. Give me your hope that surpasses all understanding. Give me your matchless peace. Even though I don't see your will, help guide me in your ways. Help me to be hopeful for your answer, letting go of my agenda. Take control, Lord. I let go of the reins. I will wait on you. Strengthen me today. Help me to be patient and joyful while waiting on you. I am ready for the next season you have for me and willing to learn what you want to show me in this season. Open my eyes to see what you would have me see. Reveal to me what you would have me to learn in this period of waiting. In your name I believe, Jesus. Amen.

I pray Day 4 ministered to you. No matter what you are facing today, or what you are waiting on, know that the Lord's answers are "yes" and "amen." Keep your hope while you wait on His next move for your life.

List ways you can be more patient while waiting on the Lord:

_____

_____

_____

_____

_____

_____

_____

_____

Day 5: Harden Not Your Heart

Today's Reading: Hebrews 3

Selected Verse for Today:

Harden not your hearts, as in the provocation, like as in the day of the trial in the wilderness.

Hebrews 3:8 (KJV)

Welcome to Day 5. Today, I want you to read Hebrews 3. I noticed in my own life that I became hardened to some people. I had to repent and ask the Lord to help me not become hardened or bitter towards others. Be careful of this. When you allow people around you or your situations to make your heart cold, you build a wall between you and God. So, today I want you to think about how you let the world around you affect who you've become. Have you become bitter or cold toward others? Have you allowed the enemy to cripple you spiritually due to a hardened heart? "Harden not your hearts," the scripture says (Hebrews 3:8, KJV). Keep a humble spirit in all manners. You are to lift one another up, not succumbing to sin through your relationships with others.

The Bible says,

Take heed, brethren, lest haply there shall be in any one of you an evil heart of unbelief, in falling away from the living God: but exhort one another day by day, so long as it is called To-day; lest any one of you be hardened by the deceitfulness of sin: for we are become partakers of Christ, if we hold fast the beginning of our confidence firm unto the end: while it is said, today if ye shall hear his voice, Harden not your hearts, as in the provocation.

Hebrews 3:12-15 (KJV)

I have been guilty of this so many times. Women especially find it hard to let things go, especially when it comes to our spouses. We tend to hold grudges and allow sin into our lives through altercations with others. The Bible says that we must forgive, otherwise, the Father won't forgive us. Holding onto bitterness is holding a grudge. If you are holding onto such things, that is unforgiveness, and you must let go. The scripture says in Hebrews not to harden your heart through deceitfulness of sin. Don't deceive yourself into thinking a grudge is okay because it isn't. The devil knows your weakness. He will tug on you in any way he can to pull you away from Christ. Any sin in your life will cause you to grow farther from the Lord. Don't allow that sin to creep in through a hardened heart. In order to stay in line with the will of God, we have to listen to Him.

I love Hebrews 8:14 (KJV) where it says that we will be partakers with Christ as long as we hold fast in our confidence until the end. So, hold fast to your confidence in Christ, don't allow the enemy to use others in your life to pull you away from the truth of God's word. Trust me, the devil will use one small thing to hinder your relationship with God. For instance, I have a friend who was offended by something someone said to her at church. She got so mad, that instead of confronting that person, she just quit coming to church. Now, what happened wasn't that bad, and I honestly didn't understand why she was offended, but she was. The devil used that situation to pull her away from the house of the Lord. We must all unite and pray for one another, being steadfast until the end! We cannot allow our hearts to become hardened to the point that we become divisive with everyone we come across.

Today's challenge is short, but I want to end with this simple illustration. The other week at church during the children's message, the teacher asked the children to name characteristics about a pack of M&M's. My son said, "They all have shells." This gave me the idea that we all have shells. Some people's shells have become hardened or bitter. Some have allowed their shells to become tainted depending on what life experience has shown them. So, today think about ways you could soften your heart. Take this time to meditate on what God would show you. Allow Him to caress your spirit with fresh insight today, breaking off any offense, wrong attitude, or pride. Ask Him to soften you heart toward others.

Let's pray.
Dear Lord,
Forgive me today for not being steadfast in your ways and for allowing the enemy to persuade me in the hour of temptation. Help me to hear your voice and open my ears to hear you clearly. I want to do your will today and every day. As I seek you today, reveal to me the places in my heart I have hardened and humble my spirit. If I have offended anyone or hardened my heart towards anyone, reveal it to me and reveal how to make it right with them. Give me your confidence to remain faithful until the end. Thank you, Lord. Amen.

It is my hope and prayer for you that your heart is softened and that today's challenge ministers to you in a powerful way. Keep pushing, my friend! It will all be worth it!

List ways you can be more humble:

_____

_____

_____

_____

_____

_____

_____

_____

Day 6: Count It All Joy

Today's Reading: James 1

Selected Verse for Today:

My brethren, count it all joy when ye fall into divers temptations.

James 1:2 (KJV)

Hello friend and welcome to Day 6. Let's jump right into today's message. Our faith is perfected through the trials of fire, through the temptations of life, and through the burdening of hardship. But as the scripture says, you are to count it all joy. Temptations, trials, and encompassing situations can be used for spiritual growth. You are to find God in the middle of them. For that is where you are stretched, molded, and plowed. It is where you are stirred. It's where you see Him move! You are to count it all for joy.

Is God your true source of joy in the midst of chaos? Is He your solid foundation in the midst of roaring waves? Or do you let the enemy rock your boat through the hour of temptation? This passage in James is so powerful. It helps reveal to the believer the foundation of truth. Meditate on James 1 today. Ask God to help you in those moments. Seek Him and His Joy. Through His joy, you will encounter His presence, His love, and His peace. So, it won't matter what storm you face, your countenance will not be changed. You will not be shaken, for His grace will shine upon you because you chose to count it all joy!

Today, I want you to look at the circumstances in your life from a different perspective. No matter how hard things may seem, find the joy in the middle of it all. Seek God's presence today and ask Him to show you His grace and His will during this time. Ask Him to give you His joy, and He will. If you can, try not to allow the enemy and others to rob your joy.

Joy is so important to our mental health, physical health and spiritual health. The Bible even says in Proverbs 17:22 (KJV) that laughter is like a dose of medicine. Try to find joy in your relationships with your spouse, your children, your friends, and co-workers. Try to find joy in the things the Lord has done for. When you find joy in the small things, you become more grateful, and when you become more grateful, the spirit of hopelessness leaves. Don't be hopeless, for that only leads to questioning God. We will never have all of the answers or know why certain things happen to us or others. Today's challenge is short and sweet, but I hope you find it meaningful. Today, try to find joy in the small things and to be grateful.

List below what you're thankful for and ask how you can change and have God's joy during this season or situation, or just in the motions of everyday life. Keep pushing!

Let's pray.
Dear Heavenly Father,
I seek you today and your joy. I seek your grace to cover me during this time. I ask that you reveal to me how I can change today. Help me to have your joy. Change my perspective. Open my eyes to see how you see, giving me wisdom and truth in the hour of temptation. I want you, Lord. Go before me and be my substance in my time of need so that no matter what I face I can count it all as joy. Thank you, Lord, for your blessings and your mercy. Thank you for your love and joy and peace that passes all understanding. I give you praise, glory and honor. In Jesus name I pray these things. Amen.

You're first week of spiritual growth is almost done. Rest in His joy today and know that through this stretching season, He is perfecting His will in you. Amen!

Day 6: Count It All Joy

Today I am joyful for:

_____

_____

_____

_____

_____

_____

_____

_____

_____

Day 7: A Lukewarm Spirit

Today's reading: Revelation 3:15-22

Selected Verse for Today:

"So then because thou art lukewarm, and neither cold nor hot, I will spue thee out of my mouth."

Revelation 3:16 (KJV)

Today, I want you to study Revelation 3:15-22. The other day as I prayed for our nation, the Holy Spirit whispered to me the word "lukewarm." I believe that the church, as a whole, needs to rise up and spread the truth of God's word like never before. So many Biblical values have been taken out of our institutions, government, and society as a whole. God is calling His church to fervently pursue Him and forsake the lukewarm spirit. As I wrote this page, the world was in the middle of the COVID-19 pandemic. Our nation was shut down for months, and so many people suffered. Businesses were shut down, church doors were closed, curfews were implemented, and people struggled financially. God spoke to me and said the pandemic was a wake-up call. It was a spiritual battle played out on a physical level. The enemy vomited filth and hatred during that chaotic time.

The Lord wants the church to be on fire for Him again. He wants each and every one of us to deal with the sins in our hearts and lives so that we can usher in revival. Ask yourself, do you want to be on fire for the kingdom of God? Do you want to set an example of Christ and be the light to others?

It's so easy to spot blatant sins the Bible refers to: fornication, drunkenness, blasphemy, gossip, idolatry. But God is speaking directly to His body, telling us to turn away from our lukewarm spirit. He says that if we are lukewarm, He will spit us out. He wants us to be on fire for Him, tried and refined in fire, purified for His Kingdom.

He says that we may go through trials and tribulations: some caused by our own decisions, some caused by the enemy, and some that He allows. Don't place blame on the Lord and distance yourself from Him, instead draw closer to Him.

He also says some of us have turned to other fleshly desires to try and fulfill the void in our lives. But He says today is the day we repent and return to Him no longer living lukewarm lives. He wants us to seek Him fervently with a zeal for Him like never before. He wants us to have a passion for Him.

Maybe you've read each day in this challenge and haven't had a God encounter yet. I pray that this day will speak to you, and that this will be the day the Holy Spirit strikes a fire in you. His word in Revelation 2:29 (KJV) says to him that have an ear, let him hear what the spirit is saying. I pray your ears may be open, that you will incline your ear to hear what the word of the Lord is saying to us today. This is a powerful word that we all need to live by. I don't want to live a lukewarm life putting other things before God. I want to seek Him daily. He says that we should have no other idols before Him. I want to dive into His word and be refined by His fire. That fire purifies us so that on the great return of the Lord, we are ready for Him, without spot or blemish! He is our groom, and we are His bride. I want to be spotless so that when He comes, He can say to me, "Well done my good and faithful servant!" Don't you want to hear that, too?

The Lord has struck a fire inside my belly, and I want that for you, too! But it won't happen if your time is occupied elsewhere. God wants you. He wants to feed you His truth, which you will only get through reading His word and spending time with Him. Binge read your Bible. Spend hours in prayer. Turn on that praise music every chance you get. This will pull the Holy Spirit into your life and chase away that lukewarm spirit.

Let's pray.

Dear Lord,

Gracious heavenly Father, forgive me for putting worldly desires above my desire to know you more. Forgive me for seeking the flesh, instead of you. Help me to make time for you daily. Stir up my spirit. Help me be a light for your glory. I want to be refined by you, purified. I seek you today, Lord. Cover me with your love and grace. I repent of all my sins. I love you, Lord. Manifest in my life daily, so that I may see your hand move in my life. Put a burning fire in my spirit for you. Give me a pure heart and clean hands. In your name I receive, Jesus. Amen.

Day 7 is done. Today was a hard day, but God laid it on my heart, and I knew I had to write it down. Let's continue to seek God today turning from our lukewarm spirits and setting our hearts on fire for Him!

Write down how you've been lukewarm:

_____

_____

_____

_____

_____

_____

_____

_____

Day 8: Seek God's Will

Today's Reading: 1 John 5

Selected Verse for Today:

And this is the confidence that we have in him, that, if we ask any thing according to his will, he heareth us:

1 John 5:14 (KJV)

Today, I want you to read 1 John 5:1-21. It's short and to the point. The verses are quite encouraging to the nature of who we are in Christ. It's easy to lose confidence in your faith when you don't see things going the way you envisioned. Your confidence shouldn't lie in yourself, but in the will of the Father. Jesus said:

Be not ye therefore like unto them: for your Father knoweth what things ye have need of, before ye ask him. After this manner therefore pray ye: Our Father which art in heaven, Hallowed be thy name. Thy kingdom come. Thy will be done in earth, as it is in heaven"

Matthew 6:8-10 (KJV)

See, God already knows your needs. You need to strengthen your confidence in Him and declare that His will be done in your life. But where do you start?

Jesus also says, "Not every one that saith unto me, Lord, Lord, shall enter into the kingdom of heaven; but he that doeth the will of my Father which is in heaven" (Matthew 7:21-23, KJV). Start with His will. His will for your life is His desire for you. His desires include believing in Jesus Christ, allowing you to walk in freedom from sin, and walk in His love toward one another. The first few versus of 1 John 5 express this. When you deflect sin from your life and lines up with the righteousness of His truth, you automatically begin to line up with the will God has for your life. Romans 8:28 (KJV) is a popular scripture verse that says, "And we know that all things worth together for good to them that love God." I do love this verse; however, many people neglect to quote the rest of the verse, which says, "to them who are the called according to His purpose." It is not for your purpose or your will that you are on this earth, but it is the will of the Father. Understanding His will has to be priority in your life, otherwise you will wander in the desert looking for water that isn't there.

Give God the steering wheel! I implore you today, to seek His will for your life. Keep in mind that He may not answer you when or how you think He should. But when the Lord answers, you will know it. Take a deep breath today. Inhale His will and exhale what you think is best. Just let go. It's okay, I promise, God's going to steer you right where He wants you to go!

Let's pray.
Abba, Father,
I seek you today. Line my steps up with your will. I want your purpose for my life, and not my own. Reveal to me your will for my life and give me the grace to see it through. Help me to walk the line you have drawn for me. Until I hear from you, give me your peace and patience. Help me to see your timing. In your name I ask, Jesus. Amen.

Day 8 is complete. I hope the scripture ministers to you. Seek the will of the Father, for it is His will that will usher in His presence.

DAY 8: SEEK GOD'S WILL

I need to allow God's will in these areas of my life:

_____

_____

_____

_____

_____

_____

_____

_____

Day 9: Spirit of Offense

Today's Reading: Matthew 24

Selected Verse for Today:

And then shall many be offended, and shall betray one another and hate one another.

Matthew 24:10 (KJV)

I wrote these words late at night after hearing promptly from the Holy Spirit to get up and write. At the time of writing this, our nation was dealing with the death of an African American who was killed by a cop. The nation was mourning the death of this man. The video of his death went viral online and people of all races rose to protest. Amongst all of this, riots and lootings broke out in major cities and downtown areas. Businesses were set on fire, and police cars were demolished. Car dealerships were vandalized, roads were blockaded by riots, while fires burned in the streets, and unrest rose. As all of this unfolded, I remembered a preaching I heard from David Wilkerson. He talked about a vision the Lord gave him on the end times. His vision included rioting, looting, and fires burning in the streets. The headlines on the news media outlets when I wrote this read "rioting," "looting," "fires" written in bold font saying "breaking news."

Our nation was in the middle of utter chaos just as we were starting to get back on our feet after being shut down from the COVID-19 pandemic. Some businesses had yet to open, and then, looters destroyed them. All of this laid heavy on my spirit. As I lie in bed that night reading the news, I began talking to God. He spoke to me and said, "Get up and write."

I had no idea what this challenge would be about. As I thought about all of the evil going on in our society, the Holy Spirit revealed to me that we were going through a season of offense. The spirit of offense rose up to cause turmoil and division in our nation. Satan was covering our nation with hate, chaos, and turmoil.

To be offended means to be trespassed upon, have a quarrel with, or accused. Being offended is one of the most common feelings people feel that leads to sin. It's one thing to be offended and then let it go. However, most people cannot do that. I am guilty of this myself, and for that, I have repented. You cannot allow the spirit of offense to overtake you to the point that you harden your heart and have unforgiveness towards one another. It will only lead to bitterness, hatred, and anger.

Jesus said we must above all love our neighbor. He said that loving one another and loving God are the two greatest commandments. Yet as I watch the news, love and kindness seem to escape our society. There is a passage of scripture where Jesus is being questioned by a multitude of people, and one man asked what the greatest commandments were. Jesus' responded saying "thou shalt love the Lord thy God with all thy heart, and with all thy soul and with all thy mind. This is the first and great commandment. And the second is like unto it, thou shalt love thy neighbor as thyself" (Matthew 22:37-39 KJV). So, where is the love? It has been lost to self. Today's culture is self-centered. Scripture even tells us that, "The love of many will wax cold" (Matthew 24:12 KJV).

I am completely guilty of being on the offensive, and I have to ask the Lord to help me let things go. When you hold onto hate, anger, and other offenses, you are not showing love. Your flesh finds it easier to hold onto things, but the scripture says you don't fight against flesh and blood. You fight in the spiritual realm. The closer you draw to the Lord, the easier it will be to let go of offense because you will be filled up on the love of Jesus. #lovethyneighbor should go viral. That should be a movement. Would that destroy the enemy, or what? It sure would help stop him in his tracks.

So, I must ask you: are you holding onto the spirit of offense? I know this is one of the longer challenges, but it is so important in your walk with Christ and how you treat others. Are you harboring any offense against your neighbor, friend, or even family member? Often times we hold offenses, even against our spouses. Those feelings hinder us from growing closer to the Lord. He wants you to release those feelings and let His love overcome all. Let go my friend. You are only hindering yourself spiritually and allowing the enemy to have a stronghold on your life.

When you allow offense to creep in and set up a home in your heart, you are giving power to Satan over your life. He then uses those feelings to control your actions, words, attitudes, and relationships. You can't give the enemy that control. He doesn't deserve it. Don't allow him to manipulate you through offenses. Don't hold a grudge or malice in your heart. That will only hinder your relationship with the Lord and the relationships around you. You aren't to live by your feelings. Feelings are fleeting, but God's love never waivers. Love isn't just a feeling, it's a choice. Today, I want you to choose love. If you've broken friendships and relationships due to the spirit of offense, make them right today. Pray about it and do as the Lord leads you. But I urge you not to let the power of offense guide you anymore. Be guided by love.

Let's Pray.
Heavenly Father,
I lay down the spirit of offense and choose love. I choose to set aside hard feelings and pride. I choose to let go of offenses. I release the power the enemy has had on me in this area of my life. In your name Jesus, I claim the power of love to take over in every relationship in my life. I speak love and blessings on my enemies and on those who've hurt me. I choose to let go of the hurt and brokenness. I choose to set aside differences, so that I can be a light to others. I ask today, Lord, that you will forgive me and help me to move forward and sin no

more. In your name I believe, Jesus. Amen.

I know this was a long challenge, but I'm so glad you stuck it out until the end. I believe when we let love rule our hearts, God sees our willingness and takes us deeper. We cannot allow the spirit of offense to rule our lives. It is my hope and prayer for you that if you have harbored this spirit, that it no longer has power over you in Jesus name.

DAY 9: SPIRIT OF OFFENSE

Offenses to let go of and how to show more love:

_____

_____

_____

_____

_____

_____

_____

_____

Day 10: Refreshing the Spirit

Today's Reading: Psalms 23

Selected Verse for Today:

The Lord is my shepherd; I shall not want. He maketh me to lie down in green pastures: He leadeth me beside the still waters. He restore the my soul: He leadeth me in the paths of righteousness for His names sake. Yea, though I walk through the valley of the shadow of death, I will fear no evil: for thou art with me; thy rod and thy staff they comfort me. Thou preparest a table before me in the presence of mine enemies: thou anointest my head with oil; my cup runneth over. Surely goodness and mercy shall follow me all the days of my life: and I will dwell in the house of the Lord forever.

Psalms 23:1-6 (KJV)

Welcome to Day 10. I am so glad you've pushed through to today. Today is my favorite day in this book so far. I encourage you to read this passage today and memorize it, if you haven't already. Write it on a notecard and carry it in your purse. Put it in your car. Make it the background on your phone. Write it on sticky notes and place the notes all over your home. Recite it over and over and declare it over your life. There is so much life and truth in these few verses. God is for His children, amen! If you claim to be a child of God, then learn this passage and claim it over your life right now. There will never be a satisfying of your soul through anything of this world except temporary gratification. True joy, refreshing, and restoration only comes from Jesus Christ.

So, let's break down these scripture verses for just a minute. The first verse says "the Lord is my shepherd; I shall not want" (Psalm 23:1, KJV). God is our shepherd, and in Him, we shall want for nothing. Amen to that! Throughout history, shepherds have gathered their flocks, moved them about, and led them to water. Shepherds must go after any of their sheep that get separated from the flock. That's what God does for you. He will chase you down and corral you back under his arms.

The next verse says, "He maketh me to lie down in green pastures; he leadeth me beside still waters" (Psalm 23:2, KJV). He leads me in green pastures and beside still waters. What do those represent? Green is a sign of wealth, abundance, good soil, and growth. Still waters represent peace. I'll take His peace and abundance any day, wouldn't you? We need to claim his peace and abundance over our lives daily, expecting to receive them! It is his peace and presence that will come and refresh us in our time of need.

Verse three, says "He restoreth my souls; he leadeth me in the paths of righteousness for his name's sake" (Psalm 23:3, KJV). Many things on a day-to-day basis can cause us to lose our temper or become upset or angry at others. Sometimes we may even feel a little beaten up or run down. We get upset over the tiniest of issues and allow the devil to disrupt our entire day. In those moments, recite this to yourself. Ask God to be your peace in those moments of testing and to restore your spirit man with a fresh anointing.

Let's look at verse four. It is profound as it says, "though I walk through the valley of the shadow of death, I will fear no evil" (Psalms 23:4, KJV). Hello! WOW! Scream that from your rooftop and make Satan mad! Have no fear, amen! That's like saying "I know I will have some rough days ahead. I know that my situation may look bleak, but I know my God's got this, and I have no fear!"

He says that His rod and His staff will comfort us. A shepherd's rod and staff are a symbol of correction and guidance. A shepherd corrects his flock and keeps them together. Don't disregard the correction of the Lord because that will lead you closer to Him, His righteous, and away from the desires of the flesh. I know it's so hard to be corrected sometimes, and we as humans don't like it. But just as a parent rewards their child for doing good after being corrected, so does the Lord reward His flock. I don't know about you, but I want to be rewarded. I want to go deeper in the spirit, but the only way that will happen is through obedience and correction. This is a hard push today, but it will be so rewarding. He will never lead you astray.

Verse five, which is probably one of my favorite verses here, says, "Thou preparest a table before me in the presence of mine enemies; thou anointest my head with oil; and my cup runneth over" (Psalms 23:5, KJV). I just want to let out a shout when I say this! The power that is in this verse is overwhelming! It takes you into a mindset of "I can do this." No matter what you are facing, you've got this!

This passage symbolizes sitting at a feast, which David did with King Saul. The Bible says that David loved the Lord, and that he was a man after God's own heart. God kept a hedge of protection around David even though he sat at the table with King Saul, who sought to kill David. This all took place even though David had already been anointed to be the next king through the prophet Samuel. Saul chased David for years, but David was always blessed and protected. God kept him safe even in the presence of his enemies. I want that protection, don't you? I want God to see that I long for Him as David did. God chooses those who are willing and faithful. God used David, and therefore David was blessed. I want that same blessing and protection. I want my cup to be full of the Holy Spirit and running over with the protection of the Lord, don't you?

As we end today, I want you to reflect on negative mindsets and speech. I want you to make a conscious effort to speak life. The Bible says the power of life and death is in the tongue. Proclaim Psalm 23 over your life daily. Glean all you can from this passage and squeeze the words like lemons. Pour them over your life and your family's lives. Proclaim God's blessings, protection, and restoration over your life. Memorize this scripture, and in your moment of temptation recite it to yourself. Ask the Lord to fill your cup with His presence and keep pushing!

Let's pray.

Dear Lord,

I thank you for your guidance and correction. I thank you for your presence. I pray that your Holy Spirit inhabit me today and every day, guiding me in the ways that I should go. I thank you for your goodness and mercy. I thank you for your protection and love. In the middle of my hardest days, I ask that your peace come and cover me like a blanket. I ask that your abundance will flood my life. I seek you today, Lord, and your presence. I ask that your presence go before me. Even in the presence of my enemies, I know that you're there keeping me safe. I ask that you restore my soul and refresh it daily like the morning dew. Let my spirit be renewed. In the name of Jesus, I pray. Amen.

Day 10 is done. I hope and pray it has ministered to you. See you tomorrow, friend. Keep pushing.

Day 10: Refreshing the Spirit

Today I speak truth over these areas of my life:

_____

_____

_____

_____

_____

_____

_____

_____

Day 11: A Proud Spirit

Today's Reading: Proverbs 16

Selected Verse for Today:

Pride goeth before destruction, and an haughty spirit before a fall.

Proverbs 16:18 (KJV)

Here we go, Day Eleven is here! I hope you are ready to dive into what God has laid on my heart for today. This isn't a subject we like to talk about, but it is relevant to our spiritual growth.

Pride can often be one of those hidden sins that you don't pay any attention to. It is often sneaky and lurks just under your prejudice, values, attitudes, and reactions. All of which are central to your walk with the Lord and your walk in this world. I remember a phone conversation I had with someone several years ago, and in that conversation, I made a rude statement about someone else. I don't remember exactly what I said, but right then I was convicted. The person on the other end said, "You know pride is a sin." At the time, I wouldn't have thought it to be pride but a rude comment. That's how slick pride can be. It sneaks around just beneath our thoughts. Without realizing it, our pride can predict the way we think or react to someone else.

So, today I want you to focus on Proverbs 16. The entire chapter is full of what I call truth bombs. Simply put, they are great revelations to live by. This chapter is full of wisdom, and you will be blessed to heed as much understanding as you can from it. The author says, "How much better it is to get wisdom that gold! And to get understanding rather to be chosen than silver" (Proverbs 16:16, KJV). I don't know about you, but I choose correction through scripture, to be chastised by the truth of the word. I want to gain wisdom and righteousness through the lens of the Lord. I hope that through this challenge God places the same desire in you.

Think about the referenced scripture at the top. The scripture goes on to say, "Pride goeth before destruction, and an haughty spirit before a fall" (Proverbs 16:18, KJV). How many times does God try to correct His children through life lessons? Instead of heeding His word, we try to accomplish our own agenda our own way. The next scripture verse says you would be better to humble yourself, then to gain any riches and divide them with the proud. With that being said, focus on uncovering the pride in your life. Ask the Lord to reveal to you today the hidden pride in your heart. I want to be humble and counted worthy, not proud and counted among the haughty and unrighteous. You also need to remember to keep a repentant heart. A repentant heart before the Lord keeps you in line with His word.

As you begin to recognize the pride in your heart, try to respond differently to others. Learn to accept and receive that where you are in life is okay. Where others are in life is okay. You are responsible for yourself, not others. How you speak, act, and respond to others will not only change the atmosphere around you, but you will also share the love of Christ through making those simple changes. Setting a Christ-like example will minister to others more than anything else you can ever do.

This passage in Proverbs is one of my favorites for gaining understanding and wisdom, both of which bring spiritual growth. Pushing out the pride in your life will bring you closer to God and allow you to recognize the sin you need to change. I hope you receive as much as I did from the passage, and that you are blessed from it.

Below, I'd like for you to write down the pride in your life. Write about things you know you need to change that represent haughty attitudes, and also write down characteristics you'd like the Lord to develop in you to have a humble spirit.

Pride to push out:

DAY 11: A PROUD SPIRIT

Let's pray.

Heavenly Father,

Help me to realize the sin in my life caused by pride. Humble my spirit and allow me to see all things in my life through your lens. Help me to show others love and mercy as you have shown me love and mercy. Show me your ways, so that I may gain understanding and wisdom. Inhabit me today, Lord. Give me a sound mind, righteous thoughts, and actions. Release the pride from my life and forgive me for having any pride or haughtiness. I ask that you forgive me of my sins and cover me with your grace, love and mercy today. In your name I ask, Jesus. Amen.

Day 11 is over! I am so glad you've kept pushing through each challenge. I hope you've seen God's hand on your life and have experienced spiritual growth. See you tomorrow!

Pride to push out:

_____

_____

_____

_____

_____

_____

_____

_____

Day 12: Mind of the Spirit

Today's Reading: Romans 8:1-16

Selected Verse for Today:

For they that are after the flesh mind the things of the flesh; but they that are after the Spirit the things of the Spirit. For the mind of the flesh is death; but the mind of the Spirit is life and peace.

Romans 8:5-6 (ASV)

In today's challenge, read Romans chapter 8:1-16. As Christians, we should constantly strive to walk closer with the Lord. In order to go deeper in Him, you have to keep pushing. Before I wrote this book, the Lord placed a desire in me to learn more about the power of the Holy Spirit. That is exactly what's up on the board for us today. When you receive Jesus as your savior, you automatically receive the presence of the Holy Spirit, yet so many people don't walk by the unction of the spirit.

A couple of years ago, I struggled with some emotional baggage. I couldn't seem to get my head above water. I tried my best to work through the anxiety I was dealing with at the time. I remember the Lord whispering to me, "Stop trying to do in the flesh what can only be done in the spirit." This was so powerful to me, and I needed to hear this truth. I tried to fight my anxiety on my own, without leaning into the Lord. I had to trust the power of the Holy Spirit to come and subdue me in those anxious moments. Have you ever felt this way? As if you can't seem to press forward and don't know why. Maybe you haven't allowed the Holy Spirit to do His job.

Most of the time, your days are spent operating in the flesh. You talk in the flesh, walk in the flesh, react in the flesh, but God wants you to walk with Him and allow the Holy Spirit to go before you. The only way to do that is by pushing out those fleshly responses. You must train yourself to allow your spirit man to react. When you aren't renewed or refreshed in the Spirit, you will more than likely react in the flesh. This can lead to negative outcomes.

So, how do you get to that place where your spirit man is built up and goes before you? Scripture says to seek the Kingdom of Heaven first and to pray without ceasing. This has to become routine for you. If you are walking in the flesh, that will be your response, but if you are walking by the spirit, that will be your response. Flesh will always be flesh, but when your Spirit is trained through the truth of the Holy Spirit, your immediate reactions will be that of love and peace. You must pray daily that the Lord will fill you with the power of His Holy Spirit, and He will. You have to practice getting in His presence and being led by the Holy Spirit if you want to walk continually in the prompts of the Holy Spirit. If you are trying to overcome anything in the flesh, such as addictions, depression, anger, forgiveness, then you've got to get in the Spirit.

Just as you live here on earth in the physical, there is a spiritual realm. Much of what you do is in the physical. God ushers you in to the spiritual, but you have to practice getting in it. There seems to be a void in many Christian lives, and I believe this is the disconnect right here. According to scripture, your battles are in the spiritual realm. So, that's what you have to do: practice getting in the spirit.

I've heard it said that humans think over fifty-thousand thoughts a day. I know that sounds insane, but if that's true, then there are fifty thousand times a day the enemy may try to steal our thoughts. If he gets your mind, he can keep you from the spirit. Start practicing experiencing the presence of the Holy Spirit. Get in a quiet place, pray, and play worship music. Set the atmosphere for the Lord to inhabit you. I believe churches aren't teaching enough on the power of the Holy Spirit, which ends up aiding in the division or void in our lives. A lot of people never see change in their lives, because they just miss out on this step. They try to do for themselves what only the Holy Spirit can do.

Day 12: Mind of the Spirit

If you've received Jesus as your Savior, then scripture says you've been filled with the Holy Spirit. You need to tap into that divine reality. Where the spirit of the Lord is, there is freedom, amen!

Many Christians never lean into this truth. They've accepted Jesus, but that's about as far as they've taken the relationship. They don't like correction, conviction, or don't want to change. They don't want to listen to the pushes of the Holy Spirit or study their Bible. My mom has always said, "You can have as much of the Lord as you want, or you can have as little as you want." How much of the Lord do you want?

There is so much that can be said on this subject; including talking about the gifts of the Spirit, but that's another book all in itself. What I want you to focus on today is reading the above referenced scripture in Romans 8. I realize your time may be limited but try in every moment you have to seek God. This is the entire purpose of this book: to push out the flesh and walk closer to Jesus. When you have more time, concentrate on getting in a room by yourself, putting on praise music, and just praying. Just bask in the presence of God. He will come and inhabit your presence.

Once you start seeing God inhabit your daily life, you will begin to see more truth. God will reveal more and more to you in the spiritual realm. So, today, practice getting in His presence. Whether it be in your car, in your living room, in your bathroom, or wherever you can be alone. If you're a mom with kids at home, put your kids down for a nap or in their rooms. If you own a business, tell your employees you will be unavailable and silence your phone. If you're older and have free time at home, make the most of that time with the Lord, your household chores can wait. Do whatever it takes to get in His presence. God wants that undivided attention. I promise you this is where so many blessings and healing in your spiritual life will come from. This is where spiritual growth blossoms. Get ready to bloom!

Let's Pray.

Dear Lord, Abba Father,

I seek you earnestly today. I ask that you forgive me of my sins and wash me clean. Show me the error of my flesh, and how to grow closer to you in the spiritual. Help me to push deeper in my relationship with you. Bring healing to my life and show me your ways. Come down and inhabit me daily. Let me see the power of your Holy Spirit move in my life. Manifest in me daily and in my prayer time. Help me to mind my spirit man. Reveal to me your will and take me deeper. Help me to glorify your name. In your name I ask, Jesus. Amen.

I hope you enjoyed today, and it is my prayer that you see the Holy Spirit move in your life. Practice getting in His presence and being moved by His Spirit like never before. Meditate on the scripture verses and ask God to show you something new in His word.

DAY 12: MIND OF THE SPIRIT

List ways to overcome the flesh through the spirit:

_____

_____

_____

_____

_____

_____

_____

_____

Day 13: Slow to Anger

Today's Reading: James 1:12-23

Selected Verse for Today:

Wherefore, my beloved brethren, let every man be swift to hear, slow to speak, slow to wrath.

James 1:19 (KJV)

Welcome to Day 13, my friend! Let's jump right it. God placed a burning in my belly to focus on the consequences of anger. We all deal with anger at some point in our lives. It is something that can rise up so quickly in our hearts, and before we know it, like a seed, it will grow and sprout into sin in our lives. As a mother, I have to restrain myself from anger when my children don't listen, and let me just say, this is super hard. Also, as a wife, when I feel as if my husband isn't listening or respecting my opinion, I have to control my anger. Controlling anger is effectively modeling self-control.

Do you express good self-control over anger, or do you let it get you into trouble sometimes? I know I let it get in the way sometimes, and I'll feel the Holy Spirit's conviction. Those weak areas in my life may be different from yours though. Think about those areas in your life where you allow anger to rise up.

Today, let's read James 1:12-23. Think about the second trimester of pregnancy. The woman's belly starts to "show," and she begins to have what people call a "glow" about her. Today's push is to work on controlling anger. Imagine that every time you exhibit self-control over this area of your life, you put on a spiritual "glow." You will have a spiritual "show" about you that others see.

This is probably one of my weak spots. But here is where I have seen blessing in my life. When I actively push down what my flesh would like to do, I feel a physical shift in my spirit. I consciously have to make a decision to respond out of love instead of anger sometimes. When I make that decision, I can literally feel myself trampling the enemy, amen! That is a better reward than anything I could ever ask for. That's what I want for you. I want you to be rewarded for choosing the spiritual over the natural. When your emotions rise, grab ahold of self-control like it's an anchor, resist the urges of the flesh, and respond in a loving manner. I know this area may be hard for you, but I promise it is where you will see an atmospheric shift.

When my attitude changes and I don't allow anger to well up inside, I physically see others around me react in a more loving way also. This is especially true in my house with my children and how we respond to one another. If you react or speak out of anger, you may cause others to react in the same way. Focus on showing love instead of anger. Keep pushing. God's got a reward for you!

Let's Pray.
Dear Lord,
Thank you for the rod of correction in my life. Thank you for your truth. I submit my whole self to you. I ask that you reveal to me the areas that provoke me to sin and anger. Give me strength in self-control, and when I want to respond with anger, quicken my spirit. Help me to have a spirit of love and to respond out of love. Help bridle my tongue so that I don't speak words of discouragement or malice to others. Please forgive me, Father, for the sins in my life. Forgive me for speaking words out of anger. Help me push the sin out of my life and let me see you move in my life today. In your name I ask, Jesus. Amen.

I know this was a rough challenge, and you're glad it's over! Just remember throughout the day to keep God's peace and reject ugly that may want to rise! Keep pushing!

Day 13: Slow to Anger

Areas of my life where I need to reject anger and show love:

_____

_____

_____

_____

_____

_____

_____

_____

_____

Day 14: Grace for Grace

Today's Reading: John 8:1-12

Selected Verse for Today:

So when they continued asking him, he lifted up himself, and said unto them, He that is without sin among you, let him first cast a stone at her.

John 8:7 (KJV)

Welcome to Day 14. You have learned so much, but God wouldn't allow me to move forward without writing this next push. He has laid this message on my heart, and it is something I've been dealing with in my own personal life. We as humans like to point the finger at others. It seems easier than looking at our own hearts, but if you haven't noticed, that is exactly what this book is about. When you focus on changing yourself for God's glory, you align yourself with the will of the Father.

Today, let's read John 8:1-12. It is the story of an adulterous woman who the scribes and Pharisees brought into the temple before Jesus to be judged. Even if you know this story well, go read it again, for there is much to be learned. I believe the Pharisees wanted to tempt Jesus and see what he would say to try and trap Him.

Could you imagine being this woman? The shame, guilt, and public ridicule she faced would have seemed almost unbearable. Could you imagine being drug into your own church, set in front of the congregation and Pastor, and exposed for your sin? You would be utterly humiliated.

The scripture says,

They say unto him, Master, this woman was taken in adultery, in the very act. Now Moses in the law commanded us, that such should be stoned: but what sayest thou? This they said, tempting him, I believe so they could accuse him. But Jesus stooped down, and with his finger wrote on the ground, as though he heard them not. So when they continued asking him, he lifted up himself, and said unto them, He that is without sin among you, let him first cast a stone at her."

John 8:4-7 (KJV)

The scriptures say Jesus bent down and began to draw in the sand. I don't know what He drew, but what this symbolizes is that He looked past her sin. I can imagine Him down on the ground with her, exchanging gazes as the Pharisees ridiculed her. Even though Jesus responded in a way they didn't expect, what He did and said spoke volumes. Often times, it's what you don't say that can be more powerful. Sometimes, less is more. You must extend grace for grace. You wouldn't want others pointing fingers at you when you sin or publicly exposing your flaws. You must give grace if you want to receive grace just as Jesus did. He tells the Pharisees he who is without sin to cast the first stone, and one by one they all left. I can only imagine the awkward silence of the woman.

We often beat ourselves up over our mistakes or look upon others in disgust for theirs. Here, we see the heart of the Father. Jesus is on the same ground level with this woman, symbolizing that He will come down to where you are. He will meet you right where you are in life, extend grace and love, and tell you to go and sin no more. Don't be burdened by your past or grieved over the sin of others. Ask Jesus for His grace for your life and to quicken your spirit when you don't want to extend grace. You must give grace to receive grace to grow spiritually. Here, you must push the bounds of what your flesh wants to do and yearn for the Spirit to change your heart and extend grace.

Recently, I had a dispute with someone who scrutinized me and my faith. I was hurt and offended. This person tried to ridicule and question me publicly on a social media platform. I responded with scripture and expressed my heart for the Lord, but that only seemed to stoke the fire. I had to ask Jesus to help me. I didn't ridicule that person; I didn't return wrong for wrong. I prayed and allowed God to move in that situation. Then, I had to leave it at that. I had to walk away without having the last word. Many times, what we'd like to have is the last word. Ever been there before?

Think about how simple Jesus was in this situation with the adulterous woman. Offer others the same grace you would like to receive. When you are humble in nature, you will attract others. If you're dealing with your mistakes, know that Jesus sees your heart. He knew the sins you would make before you made them. He is on the ground level with you, waiting on you to look upon Him so that He can look at you and say, "Go and sin no more."

If you would but look to Jesus in every moment and realize that He is right there with you, it would be much easier to go and sin no more. So, do that today. Focus on the grace of Jesus, realize that He's forgiven you, and extend that same grace to others instead of correcting or comparing others around you. Focus on scripture and how Jesus would handle the situation. Don't walk in condemnation or condemning others, and you will feel as if a burden has been lifted off of your chest when you do so.

Today I want to end things a little different. I want to speak and pray a release over your life. If you have felt ridiculed, embarrassed, ashamed, guilty, or if you've been the accuser, I want to speak a prayer of release and grace over you right now.

Let's pray.
Dear Jesus,
As I come before you right now, I lift up those that read this scripture needing release from any bondage in their life. I speak the power of release over judgment, shame, guilt, oppression, and self-condemnation. I speak the power of healing into your life and into

your heart right now. I speak the blood of Jesus over you right now, that you will be filled with the power of the Holy Spirit to overcome any situation in your life that is holding you back from seeing God's grace. I bless you right now in the name of Jesus, receive His grace and proclaim it. Amen.

As we end today's challenge, I want you to remind yourself throughout the day to ask the Lord to help you live by His standard of grace. No matter what you're dealing with or have dealt with in the past, you are God's creation, you are loved, and you are His called according to His purpose. Ask Him to help you be a better wife, mother, daughter, sister, friend, and all that apply. Ask Him to cover you with His grace.

Day 14: Grace for Grace

How I can extend more grace:

_____

_____

_____

_____

_____

_____

_____

_____

_____

Day 15: Blessings in Obedience

Today's Reading: 2 Kings 2:1-15

Selected Verse for Today:

This book of the law shall not depart out of thy mouth; but thou shalt meditate therein day and night, that thou mayest observe to do according to all that is written therein: for then thou shalt make thy way prosperous, and then thou shalt have good success

Joshua 1:8 (KJV)

Welcome to Day 15. It is my hope and prayer that you have been ministered to thus far. I pray that you have seen the Holy Spirit move in your life. As you start today's push, I want you to know that I was emotional until God allowed this message to be released from me. While I wrote this, I fasted and prayed earnestly for His hand to move in my life so that I may be obedient to Him in all I do. I didn't want to miss out on His will and His purpose. Sometimes it's hard to submit, but when you do, no matter how long it takes, He will bless your obedience.

If you are struggling with anything that the Lord has laid on your heart, release it today and be set free. I promise that He will pour out His blessings upon you when you do that! I want you to seek God today and ask Him if that is something you need to do. During my two-week fast, I submitted myself physically, by giving up foods I love. I gave up soda, sugar, and junk food. If you know me, then you know I love cola and chocolate. Hand me a cola and a bag of M&Ms, and I'm one happy girl. Seriously though, I needed a break-through in a few areas of my life. The Lord called me to this fast. Even though it was hard, I knew His glory was just on the other side of it, and I couldn't wait! He ministered to me and said, "Do you want a piece of the pie or the whole thing?" When He spoke this into my spirit, I was so awe struck. I wanted to shout, "Yes, Lord! I want all of you, the whole pie!" If it takes me sacrificing my wants and seeking the Lord more every day to see His glory, then that's just what I'll do!

Maybe you feel led to fast sweets, certain foods, drinks, television, social media, etc. Social media can sometimes be consuming. Make sure nothing is taking up too much real estate in your life. God is a jealous God and wants to be placed above all other things. Whatever God puts on your heart to set aside, be obedient to what He convicts you of. I promise that you will see a spiritual break-through in your life.

I pray that the spirit of truth will minister to you today as you read Joshua 1. In this passage we see Joshua's dedication and obedience. If you read the entire book of Joshua, you will read about the countless battles he fought to secure the lands promised by Moses. When God asks you to do something, submit and do it. Look at what He gives afterwards. His word promises you blessings after obedience.

I recently read the story of Elijah and Elisha in 2 Kings. Their story ministered to me in such a powerful way. The prophet Elijah was a powerful man of God who called Elisha to come along with him. Elijah and Elisha moved from town to town ministering. In 2 Kings 2, we see this passage among the two prophets:

And it came to pass, when they were gone over, that Elijah said unto Elisha, Ask what I shall do for thee, before I be taken away from thee. And Elisha said, I pray thee, let a double portion of thy spirit be upon me. And he said, Thou hast asked a hard thing: nevertheless, if thou see me when I am taken from thee, it shall be so unto thee; but if not, it shall not be so. And it came to pass, as they still went on, and talked, that, behold, there appeared a chariot of fire, and horses of fire, and parted them both asunder; and Elijah went up by a whirlwind into heaven. And Elisha saw it, and he cried, My father, my father, the chariot of Israel, and the horsemen thereof. And he saw him no more: and he took hold of his own clothes, and rent them in two pieces. He took up also the mantle of Elijah that fell from him, and went back, and stood by the bank of Jordan; And he took the mantle of Elijah that fell from him, and smote the waters, and said, Where is the Lord God of Elijah? and when he also had smitten the waters, they parted hither and thither: and Elisha went over.

2 Kings 2:9-14 (KJV)

When the Lord took up Elijah by a whirlwind, a double portion of His spirit was poured out onto Elisha. Elisha put on Elijah's mantle and parted the waters of the Jordan river. How powerful is that? I believe it was Elisha's obedience that allowed him to receive the double portion. This scripture ministered to me in such a profound way that I literally mulled it over in my spirit for several weeks. Elisha followed Elijah, to do the work of the Father and out of obedience he was blessed spiritually.

That's what I want: a double portion of the Holy Spirit through obedience to His word. Read the words of the prophets, the stories of the patriarchs, the promises in Psalms, and the red words in the gospels. Be obedient and the Lord will bless you spiritually. It is my prayer that you will yearn for His truth by reading His word.

As you end today, be obedient to what God is asking of you. The reward is far greater than the sacrifice. I pray that you will be encouraged today. And ask the Lord to give you strength and courage to lay down what He asks and He will be your rod and staff.

Let's Pray.
Dear Heavenly Father,
I seek you today and your will. Whatever you would like for me to lay down in submission to you, I ask that you reveal it to me. Help me, Lord. Give me your strength, courage, and endurance to lay down the natural, so that I may increase in the spiritual. Keep me from temptation. May your will be done in my life as it is in heaven. I submit all of me in obedience to you today. And help me not to boast

or become weary in well-doing. I want to be obedient out of love for you. Forgive me of my sins, Father. And I thank you, Lord. In your name I ask, Jesus. Amen.

As we end Day 15, I want you to tell the Lord you want the whole pie. Sincerely from your heart, tell the Lord you won't be satisfied with just a little slice. And above all, be obedient to what He may ask you to do to receive the whole pie!

Day 15: Blessings in Obedience

What I am sacrificing today:

_____

_____

_____

_____

_____

_____

_____

_____

_____

Day 16: You Are Enough

Today's Reading: Proverbs 31:10-31

Selected Verse for Today:

Whatever is good and perfect is a gift coming down to us from God our Father, who created all the lights in the heavens. He never changes or casts a shifting shadow. He chose to give birth to us by giving us his true word. And we, out of all creation, became his prized possession

James 1:17-18 (NLT)

Hello friend, I am glad you've made it to Day 16! Trust me, as I've said before, I walked out every push in this book. I walked through every situation and muddy water to put these words on the page. I hope it's been a little bit easier for you than it has been for me, but God laid this book on my heart with purpose though. He wants you to experience Him like never before and see His glory. However, you can't get there without a little bit of correction and spiritual growth. So, keep pushing!

With that being said, I knew the Lord wanted me to share with you this one little phrase, "You are enough." And, you are. You are enough. Say this to yourself, "I am enough," as many times as needed. When you feel discouraged in your walk with the Lord or as if you can't seem to get things right, repeat that to yourself. You will never be perfect, and that's okay. Don't allow the enemy to rob you of your birthright. You are enough. You are good. You are loved. You are the chosen bride of Christ.

As I sought and cried out to God while writing, He spoke these words into my spirit, "It is my immeasurable cup of love that sustains." He ministered so much encouragement to me this week through that one little phrase. How powerful is that? His love is immeasurable, and to know that He graciously pours it out on me daily is more than I can fathom. May you know that it's through His love that anything can be overcome, chains can be broken, doors can open, and you can walk in freedom. The power of His love sustains, not the love of others or material things. The cares of others will not sustain, but only His love. Everything else will leave your cup empty. But His immeasurable cup of love will sustain you.

I am guilty of caring too much about what others think of me. Is that you too? This can hinder our thoughts, actions, and words, allowing the enemy to sneak his way into how we feel about ourselves. I have to work really hard not to allow the enemy to have rule over my thoughts about myself or else I criticize myself constantly. I think as women, wives, and mothers we especially seem to do this. We want to be perfect in every arena of life. We want to look like the trophy wife, the woman who gets the mom of the year award: looking beautiful and flawless while doing it. The truth of all of this responsibility is hard. It's too high a standard, right? I can't take care of the kids, cook every meal, satisfy my husband, keep a clean house, and socialize all at the same time. It is just plain impossible to keep it all together all the time.

I've had to learn that it's okay to be imperfect. No matter where I am in life, and no matter where you are in life, it's okay to miss a beat here and there. I know God loves me, and He loves you. Actually, when you are imperfect, that's when you see God's hand the most. God doesn't miss a game. When you allow Him into every area of your life, He will be there cheering you on. It is His immeasurable cup of love that sustains you throughout every season.

God knit you in your mother's womb for His purpose, to establish His righteousness in your life. He loves you unconditionally. His love for you will never waiver or falter. Walk in confidence of His love for you. You are His prized possession, and remember you are enough!

Let's Pray.

Dear Heavenly Father,

I thank you for your love today. I thank you for sending your son to die for me. Help me to see my value in who you've called me to be. I want to walk in your ways and do what you've called me to do. Help me to walk in love. I am good enough because you created me. You knit me in my mother's womb. I am your first fruit. Continue to mold and shape me into the called according to your purpose. In your name I pray, Lord. Amen.

Today was short and sweet, and I hope to the point. Know that Jesus loves you beyond anything you could imagine. He did die an unimaginably cruel death so that you could be set free. When you feel inadequate, say to yourself, "I am enough."

List positive attributes about yourself (for example: *I'm a good mother, wife and friend*):

_____

_____

_____

_____

_____

_____

_____

_____

_____

Day 17: The Power of Encouraging Others

Today's Reading: Matthew 22:37-39

Selected Verse for Today:

Jesus said unto him, Thou shalt love the Lord thy God with all thy heart, and with all thy soul, and with all thy mind. This is the first and great commandment. And the second is like unto it, Thou shalt love thy neighbour as thyself

Matthew 22:37-39 (KJV)

Let's jump right in. Day 17 is extremely relevant to what's going on in our world today. Today, you are going to delve into encouraging one another. Recently, I had a friend speak some endearing words of encouragement to me, and she prayed over me. Oh how that refreshed my spirit and gave me peace. To have someone else on the boat with you makes it easier to weather the storm. When someone gives you encouragement, it lifts the heaviness. Jesus said the greatest commandment is to love God and then next to it, to love thy neighbor.

In a world where there is so much strife and division, it is a blessing to others when you lift them up. Paul wrote, "And let us consider one another to provoke unto love and to good works: Not forsaking the assembling of ourselves together, as the manner of some is; but exhorting one another: and so much the more, as ye see the day approaching" (Hebrews 10:24-25, KJV). As we see tensions increasing in the world around us and people turning against one another, let's do the opposite and encourage our brothers and sisters. I know it's hard to do when you're the one needing encouragement, but when you go the extra mile for someone else, you will be blessed.

Think about any friends or family members that may be in need. Maybe you just come across someone in a checkout line who's having a bad day and needs uplifting. Whatever the case may be, take a moment of your time to be a friend and encourage them. The Bible says, "A man that hath friends must shew himself friendly: and there is a friend that sticketh closer than a brother" (Proverbs 18:24, KJV). These words could not be more true. We all need one another. Even in the midst of your busy life, make the time to go the extra mile. You never know how God may minister to you or the other person for showing an act of kindness.

The Lord wants to stretch you through your relationships and friendships. He wants to see what you will do for others. You never know whose life you may change just by speaking a word of encouragement or praying over them. As simple as it may sound, dropping a nice comment on someone's page on social media could change that person's day. Make an effort to be the person you want others to be to you. Make those nice gestures and comments, give compliments, and encourage other's through words, actions, or gifts. Let others know they are loved. Encouraging others is a blessing to the giver and the receiver. And scripture says the Lord loves a cheerful giver. If you're going to be on God's radar, be on it for doing something good.

So, today is short and to the point. Take the extra time to think of something nice you can do to encourage someone else who may need it.

Let's pray.
Dear Jesus,
Thank you for showing me your love. Thank you for meeting me where I am and always encouraging me. Help me to do the same for others. Reveal to me how you want me to be a good steward and serve others. When you quicken my spirit, I will be obedient. I want to show others your love. Send me someone to encourage today. In your name, Jesus. Amen.

I hope today you are encouraged and that you take the time to encourage someone else. You never know who may need it. Be the light and keep pushing

Day 17: The Power of Encouraging Others

Ways to encourage others:

_____

_____

_____

_____

_____

_____

_____

_____

Day 18: Surrender It All

Today's Reading: Jonah 1

Selected Verse for Today:

But Jonah got up and went in the opposite direction to get away from the Lord. He went down to the port of Joppa, where he found a ship leaving for Tarshish. He bought a ticket and went on board, hoping to escape from the Lord by sailing to Tarshish.

Jonah 1:3 (NLT)

As I was preparing to write this message, I was amazed at how the Lord revealed certain things to me. I was on the way to church the other morning when God laid on my heart the burning message of surrender. He said so many people want to straddle the fence. They want to do what they want to do, instead of heed the entire truth of His word. He then spoke clearly to me and said, "I am not a God of convenience; I am the God of righteousness." I began to cry in my car on the way to church at how powerful this word was. I said, "Lord, forgive me for only wanting what's convenient for me." I began to repent and surrender the parts of my heart I thought I could hide from the Lord. You can't hide anything. God knows everything. Have you ever tried to hide something from the Lord because it wasn't convenient to give it up? Usually it is the convenient things that need to go, and we must be obedient to those convictions.

I was speaking to someone last week, and she said, "I feel distant from the Lord, as if He's not hearing my prayers. So, I began to repent. Then the next day I felt a lot better." See, God wants you to surrender all of yourself to Him. He wants you to expose every part of your heart to Him. The raw parts are the hardest to deal with because they seem so painful, but those are the parts God wants to deal with. You need to stop trying to put a bandage over your issues and simply succumb to the will of the Father. Those raw places are where God does His greatest work in your life. He doesn't want you living in the shadows trying to hide. He is the God of the visible and the invisible. He wants all of you so that He can perform His perfect will. When you expose yourself to Him, communicate with Him, and nurture your relationship with Him, you grow stronger.

Take a look at Jonah. We all know this story so well, but it has so much relevance to your daily life. You see, Jonah didn't want to surrender to what God was asking him to do, and that got him into a lot of trouble. This may sound like a lot, but the chapters are short, and the scripture reads quickly. Please read the book of Jonah, chapters one through four. Yes, all four chapters, even if you have to read in spurts throughout the day. God wants you to study this story and what happened between Him and Jonah. When Jonah tried to run from God, there were consequences.

As you read toward the end of the first chapter, you see God's plan unfold. After the storm has compassed the ship that Jonah is on, the scripture says, "Now the Lord had arranged for a great fish to swallow Jonah. And Jonah was inside the fish for three days and three nights" (Jonah 1:17, NLT). How often do we reject the will of God and end up like Jonah in a tangled mess? If you would but surrender when He asks you, your story would read much differently. But God knows what you will do with what He gives you, and the scripture says, "the Lord had arranged" (Jonah 1:17, NLT). See, God arranges everything. He is the master author of everything. When you don't adhere to what He asks of you, He has other arrangements. I often wonder what those arrangements would be if I had of chosen to surrender certain areas of my life to God sooner.

After Jonah responds the second time to God's will, He goes to Nineveh and warns the people that if they don't repent, God will destroy their city. The people were obedient and ultimately saved due to Jonah's warning. How powerful is that? When Jonah decided to do what the Lord had asked him to do, an entire city was saved! Not only did Jonah do what was right, but the people also surrendered themselves to the Lord. They fasted, prayed, and made sacrifices to the Lord. Just think what could happen in your life if you did what the Holy Spirit asked of you. Think about the impact you could make in the Kingdom of God if you listened to His nudges, whispers, and pushes. Think about how you could change other people's lives by being an example for Christ.

When you surrender and stop straddling the fence, God moves mountains. When you surrender everything, you see God's purpose come full circle. If you are dealing with anything today, that you know you need to surrender to the Lord, no matter how hard it is, do it. Ask the Lord for His strength and you will overcome. The Bible says, "He giveth power to the faint; and to them that have no might, he increase strength" (Isaiah 40:29, KJV). Jonah didn't want to do what God was asking of Him. Jonah thought that what God had asked him to do would be too hard. In the flesh, it would absolutely seem impossible. But all things are possible through Christ who gives us strength, amen! So, stop straddling the fence and push forward today on whatever God asks of you. He will already have it all arranged for you. If you're unsure of anything in particular, just ask the Holy Spirit to quicken your spirit. Ask Him for His purpose, and He will show it to you.

Let's pray.
Dear Heavenly Father,
I thank you, Lord for your will and what you have asked of me to do. I know that I am your child, and that you will equip me to do what you've called me to do. I can't do anything without your strength, Lord, and I ask that you strengthen me today. I surrender to you today. I lay it all down at your feet. I expose my heart to you today, Lord. I expose the sin of my flesh. Help me to cut off the will of my flesh to do what you're asking me to do. I don't want to straddle the

fence any longer. In all my ways I acknowledge you. I love you, Lord and thank you for your will. In Jesus name I pray, amen.

After today is done, and you have spoken to the Lord, follow through and be faithful to what He has laid on your heart. Whatever He quickens inside of you to do, follow through, and you will be blessed.

Day 18: Surrender It All

Ways to surrender:

_____

_____

_____

_____

_____

_____

_____

_____

_____

Day 19: Seek Wisdom

Today's Reading: Proverbs 4

Selected Verse for Today:

Get wisdom, get understanding: forget it not; neither decline from the words of my mouth. Forsake her not, and she shall preserve thee: love her, and she shall keep thee.

Proverbs 4:5-6 (KJV).

Much of what we do, as I have said before, is in the flesh. We try to do things our own way, in our own time, and the way we think we should. We react and speak in a fleshly way. The more we are refined by the wisdom of God, the more our ways, thoughts, and speech will change to reflect that of the Lord. As I sought the Lord for today's message, He laid this scripture on my heart. If you would but seek His wisdom, you would know what to say and do. This verse says that the Lord gives it generously, and I don't know about you, but I need as much of His wisdom as I can get!

For hundreds of years, society has tried to seek knowledge and wisdom through worldly channels, such as horoscopes, mediums, sorcery, witchcraft, etc. But that is not the place to look. In fact, the Lord says, "Do not defile yourselves by turning to mediums or to those who consult the spirits of the dead. I am the Lord your God" (Leviticus 19:31, NLT). There are several scripture verses that warn us against such things. You absolutely will not find wisdom in things of the world. So many people think it's innocent to consult horoscopes, and things alike, but it is the work of darkness. The Bible says, "And have no fellowship with the unfruitful works of darkness, but rather reprove them. For it is a shame even to speak of those things which are done of them in secret" (Ephesians 5:11-12, KJV).

God is not a God of the dark but the God of light. He sent His son to show you what that light would look like in the flesh. You have to operate in the light and have no part in the darkness, for the dark is where the enemy operates. If you even entertain the thought of reaching out into darkness, that is what will return to you: darkness. The only wisdom you must seek is the Lord's.

My husband and I were discussing something the other night as we ate dinner together. He said he didn't know what to do about a certain situation, and I said, "Well, we need to pray about it." How many times do we neglect to seek God's wisdom? So, that's todays challenge. Let's study scripture and see what the Lord says if we would just seek His wisdom.

There are over two hundred scripture references about wisdom, so I'd say that wisdom is pertinent to our walk with Christ. The Bible says, "Forsake her not, and she shall preserve thee: love her, and she shall keep thee" (Proverbs 4:6, KJV). Proverbs 4 is full of instruction and wisdom. It goes on to say that you will be honored and exalted when you embrace the wisdom of God. God's wisdom holds the keys to life. I want life and life abundantly, amen!

Push out the mischief and uncertainty of what the world offers. The world will always return to the ways of the world, not the wisdom of God. Push towards the prize of God's understanding, instruction, and wisdom and gain another foothold in the spiritual. Cut out the darkness and run to the light. Run to the wisdom of the Lord.

Let's pray.
Dear Lord,
I thank you for your instruction and wisdom. I thank you for your words of truth. I thank you for the understanding of light against the darkness. I only want to live by your light, Lord. Help me to seek you first and your wisdom, not the wisdom of the world. Help me to share your light and wisdom of your truth with others. Forgive me for not always coming to you first. I bless your name, Lord. And I love you. In Jesus name I pray, amen.

We are almost done. There are only a couple of days left. I hope and pray that today ministered to you. I pray that you seek God's wisdom for your life. No matter what situation you are facing, I pray that you will not be confused for confusion is of the devil. I pray that you will have the Lord's peace in your life right now. Wait upon the Lord, and like Solomon, I pray you will receive divine wisdom from the Lord.

List ways to seek God's wisdom:

_____

_____

_____

_____

_____

_____

_____

_____

Day 20: Sow Righteousness, Reap Mercy

Today's Reading: Hosea 10

Selected Verse for Today:

Sow to yourselves in righteousness, reap in mercy; break up your fallow ground: for it is time to seek the Lord, till he come and rain righteousness upon you.

Hosea 10:12 (KJV)

Welcome to Day 20! You are almost done, but I know God isn't even close to being finished with you! God ministered to me the other day this truth. He said, "I am not a God of convenience but the God of righteousness." Your situation and circumstances may not be convenient, but God doesn't often work in the middle of convenience. God works in the areas of your life that are most uncomfortable. He wants to work in your life through your circumstances. You are who God says you are, and you must follow Him. You cannot follow the world, for it will always lead to destruction. If by this point you haven't been pulled out of your comfort zone, God isn't done pushing you through this challenge. This book may offend, it may call out your sins, as it has mine, but that is its purpose. God wants to push us closer to Him through seeking righteousness.

As I studied my Bible while writing, I read Hosea 10:12. It stood out to me. It confirmed what God was already ministering to my spirit about His righteousness. He has whispered the word righteousness into my spirit over the past couple of weeks. When God whispers to us, it is so encouraging.

Hosea says to "sow righteousness and reap mercy" (Hosea 10:12, KJV). How powerful is that? If you would but seek righteousness, you would reap mercy. How many times have you heard, "You reap what you sow"? What seeds have you been planting? Have they been seeds of righteousness?

As you see in this passage of scripture, Israel will reap what they sow. They turned to the world instead of God's righteousness, and the hand of God's judgment was on them. I don't know about you, but I don't ever want to be caught seeing the world's ways over the Lord's.

I like to think about my walk with the Lord as a spiritual measurement. Some days the measurement feels shorter and other days it feels longer. If you could be spiritually measured today, what would that measurement look like? I hope that through this challenge, you have been spiritually stretched. I hope and pray that your measurement has been lengthened, and that you've seen God's mercy in your life. I know I need God's mercy!

As I studied this scripture verse, I looked up the meaning of the word fallow. It means to be uncultivated, not pregnant, and infertile. It also can refer to "land that has undergone plowing and harrowing and has been left unseeded for one or more growing seasons" (dictionary.com).

My husband has a tractor he uses to plow our garden. His plow and harrows are what he uses to dig and turn the soil over before we plant our garden. The harrows till up the topsoil and turn over the dirt that's been buried beneath. The dirt then looks dark and richer. We then let it sit for a few weeks before we plant our garden. Any farmer will be the first to tell you how important your soil is. If you don't have nutrient rich soil, your garden won't flourish. It is my prayer that your spiritual soil has been plowed and harrowed and ready to be planted with new seeds of righteousness. I want you to reap in God's mercy. I want you to receive God's mercy, favor, and heavenly reward. Now that your spiritual ground is tender and turned over, get ready for the new seeds God is about to plant in your life. The seeds of righteousness are in wait, and in due season you will reap in mercy.

Let's pray.

Dear Merciful Heavenly Father,

I thank you for your mercy, Lord. I thank you for your righteousness. I ask that you cultivate in me new seeds of righteousness. Minister to me through your word and truths so that in due season I may reap in your mercies for they are renewed every morning. I thank you, Father, for your love for me and for what you are going to do in my life during this season. Fertilize my spiritual soil with your grace, love, compassion and mercy, so that I may grow in them. Help me to exhibit your mercy toward others. In your name I ask, Jesus. Amen.

We're almost done, and I am so excited for what God is doing in your life and for what He is going to do. See you tomorrow!

IVY SMITH

Write down ways you've seen God's mercy in your life:

_____

_____

_____

_____

_____

_____

_____

_____

Day 21: Guard Your Heart

Today's Reading: Proverbs 4

Selected Verse for Today:

"Guard your heart above all else, for it determines the course of your life.

Proverbs 4:23 (NLT)

I am so glad you've made it to Day 21. I know you've addressed some hard issues, but you can't change what you don't confront. God gives spiritual blessings to those who continually seek Him. I hope these past few weeks have sparked a revival in your spirit!

The first day of this book talked about examining your heart, and God has brought this twenty-one-day journey full circle with this last message. He laid this scripture on my heart, and I immediately knew that this was how He wanted me to end the book. Read Proverbs 4 and see how you are to guard your heart.

So, what does it say? The scripture says you should guard your heart, for out of your heart are the issues of life. If your heart is empty or full of filth, you cannot do what God calls you to do. But when you guard your heart, protect it from the lies of the enemy, sustain it through the truth of the word, you have the ultimate victory. It is only when you let your guard down that sin can creep in allowing division between you and God. You cannot afford any division between you and God! You must be able to fight the enemy with scripture and guard your heart against the wiles of the devil. You see here the scripture says not to lose sight of God's word for it is as health to the body. Some translations say health to the bones. God's word is the truth that fights the lies of the enemy. It is sharper than any two-edged sword, amen!

So how do you guard your heart? You guard your heart by using spiritual weapons through seeking God's word, spending time with

Him in praise and worship, and praying. Incline your ear to hear from the Lord and by doing such things. You will create a spiritual protective shell around your heart. The thicker the shell, the harder it is for the enemy to break in.

Paul writes,

"The night is far spent, the day is at hand: let us therefore cast off the works of darkness, and let us put on the armour of light. Let us walk honestly, as in the day; not in rioting and drunkenness, not in chambering and wantonness, not in strife and envying. But put ye on the Lord Jesus Christ, and make not provision for the flesh, to fulfill the lusts thereof"

(Romans 13:12-14, KJV).

This scripture is so profound to me. Put on the armor of light, that is Jesus Christ! When you put on that armor, you are in essence guarding your heart against the wiles of the enemy.

If you knew that you were going into battle, you would do all you could to put on physical armor to protect yourself. That's what you have to do in the spiritual realm. You must pick up your spiritual weapons to slay the enemy. If you haven't pulled out your spiritual weapons to fight your battles, you will lose. Guard your heart with all diligence, picking up spiritual weapons to fight your battles. Daily, you must put on the armor of God.

Put on the whole armor of God that ye may be able to stand against the wiles of the devil. For we wrestle not against flesh and blood, but against principalities, against powers, against the rulers of the darkness of this world, against spiritual wickedness in high places. Wherefore take unto you the whole armor of God, that ye may be able to withstand in the evil day, and having done all, to stand. Stand therefore, having your loins girt about with truth, and having on the breastplate of righteousness; And your feet shod with the preparation of the gospel of peace; Above all, taking the shield of faith, wherewith ye shall be able to quench all the fiery darts of the wicked. And take the helmet of salvation, and the sword of the Spirit, which is the word of God: Praying always with all prayer and supplication in the Spirit, and watching thereunto with all perseverance and supplication for all saints.

Ephesians 6:11-18, (KJV)

Push and prepare yourself for your daily life by picking up spiritual weapons. Fight daily, preserving your life in the paths of righteousness. And, yes, you will walk through plenty of valleys, but God is with you, amen! His rod and His staff will comfort you. So, pick up your spiritual weapons and fight the enemy with truth, righteousness, peace, faith, scripture, prayer, and supplication, enduring until the end. Incline your ear to hear the Lord. Obey the quickening of the Holy Spirit. Listen to His whispers, His nudges, and even His pushes. And, remember this, you have the victory, amen!

I want to us to end today, the final day, making this proclamation. Say it out loud, believing it and claiming it.

I am a child of God. I am a daughter of the one true King. I am a city on a hill. I will shine my light in the darkness. I will walk in the ways of the Lord. I am blessed and favored. I am protected. I am called according to His purpose. I am loved. I am free from sin. My reward is not on this Earth but in Heaven. And I will praise the name of Jesus forever. I love you, Lord. I give you all the glory and honor and praise. I thank you for this spiritual challenge. I thank you for what you are doing in my life and for what you are going to do. I can't wait to go deeper in your love and mercy. Fill me today, Holy Spirit, with your conviction and power. Let me see your manifest presence in my life. Continue to push me so that I may walk closer with you. Birth something new in me so that I may walk in your light and will for my life during this season. In your name I believe, Jesus. Amen.

Congratulations! Your twenty-one-day journey is finished, but I know God isn't nearly done pushing you! Over the last few weeks you've examined your heart, pulling out the dirty laundry so to speak. God's given you fresh, revelatory truths. You've pursued His word and His righteousness. You've exposed the raw and painful places in your heart. You've replaced the ugly with fresh insight. Over the last few weeks, you've discovered God's grace, love, and mercy. God has revealed to you how to listen to His whispers, nudges, and even pushes. I hope and pray that like a radio station, you've learned to dial Him in more clearly. The noise isn't scratchy, but crystal clear. I hope that you've made a routine of reading God's word, sacrificing a few moments of your day to spend time with Jesus. It is my hope and prayer that this book led you closer to the Lord. I pray that you will be blessed. I pray that through this challenge you've seen God move in your life. The book is over, but the rest of the challenge lies within you. Keep pushing, my friend, and be blessed in the name of Jesus.

Bibliography

"Dictionary.com." 2020 Dictionary.com. 4 September 2020 <http://www.dictionary.com/browse/fallow?s=t>

About the Author

Ivy Smith is a wife and mother, seeking to encourage other women. She lives in the Upstate of South Carolina. Ivy and her husband, David are raising their two sons, Samuel and Gabriel.

CPSIA information can be obtained
at www.ICGtesting.com
Printed in the USA
BVHW060715130121
597635BV00004B/12

9 781647 737399